Across The Unseen

From Serendipity to Forever : A 21-Poem Love Tale

Suchita Sarcar Ghosh

BookLeaf Publishing
India | USA | UK

Made with ❤ on the BookLeaf Publishing Platform
www.bookleafpub.in
www.bookleafpub.com

Dedication

To My Dearest Husband - **Aveek**, in every word and verse of this collection, our love story unfolds. From the first moment we met to the quiet, everyday moments we share, you are the inspiration behind every line and every rhyme. This book is a monument to our love, which becomes stronger with each passing day. Thank you for being my muse, my partner, and my most exciting experience.

Preface

Through verses of joy, reflection, and growth, this book captures the essence of a bond that was forged not only by choice but by an undeniable sense of being meant for one another. In a world where love often feels like a serendipitous encounter, our story began with the careful, deliberate steps of an arranged marriage. Yet, within the framework of tradition, we discovered a love so profound and enduring that it transcended the confines of fate. As you read these poems, I invite you to experience the magic of our journey—the blending of destiny and devotion, the strength found in vulnerability, and the unspoken language of love that flourishes even in the most structured beginnings. May these words resonate with those who have walked similar paths, and may they inspire all who seek to find the remarkable in the seemingly predestined.

Acknowledgements

As I compose and prepare these words, I am overwhelmed with gratitude to everyone who has contributed to this artistic venture. My dear husband, your unwavering love, support, and inspiration have been the driving force behind this book. Thank you, family and friends, for your encouragement and patience as I plunged myself in the realm of words. Thank you to everyone who picks up this book and allows these poems to find a place in their hearts. I hope they resonate with you as much as the situations that inspired them do with me. Every line in these poems captures a piece of my heart. Thank you to everyone who has been a part of this journey; without your support and love, this collection would not have been existed.

1. A Request under the Stars

After birthday lights had dimmed,
And echoes of laughter softly skimmed.
In the calm of a night so still,
A message arrived, unexpected thrill.

On Shaadi.com, an interest sparked,
Amidst post-party warmth, it marked.
A gentle nudge from fate's own hand,
A new chapter yet to be planned.

In the haze of celebration's glow,
I paused, unsure, the seeds to sow.
Yet as September's 9th dawned clear,
A thought emerged from deep sincere.

With a heart now open, free from doubt,
The request was met, a gentle shout.
Acceptance breathed through every line,
A step towards what could be divine.

2. September's Afternoon

On September's 9th, beneath the afternoon's gentle gaze,
A chat sparked life in a serendipitous daze.
Numbers exchanged in a moment so light,
A bridge of digits igniting the night.

From screens to the heart, the connection so clear,
A whisper of chance in the digital sphere.
Facebook's embrace welcomed us with grace,
A new thread of conversation, a familiar face.

"Hi" on WhatsApp, a greeting so small,
Yet in those simple words, a new story would sprawl.
Chats blossomed slowly, introductions took flight,
In the quiet of evening, our worlds felt so right.

Normal joys and hobbies began to intertwine,
In each shared moment, a hint of design.
September's afternoon had begun our quest,
In the world of ones and zeros, we found something blessed.

3. Planning the Confluence

We shared our parents' numbers, a bridge we laid,
Their voices connected through thoughtful calls,
To find a place where our futures could cascade,
And set a meeting where harmony befalls.

After long discussions and careful thought,
My rental home was chosen in Sambalpur's grace,
Where new beginnings and traditions were caught,
As Balasore's festive spirit found its place.

In October's festive cheer, you journeyed from Kolkata,
To celebrate Durga's might on ancestral grounds,
And once Laxmi Puja's glow began to scatter,
Our weekend gathering in calm would resound.

With eager hearts, we looked forward to that day,
When our families would gather and paths intertwine,
In the gentle warmth where futures would softly play,
And the glow of tomorrow would begin to define.

4. Echoes of Our First Call

In the quiet before our eyes could meet,
A message blinked, a pulse of fleeting beat,
"Should I call you?" it softly said,
A longing plea, with hope widespread.

The phone's ring broke the stillness like a wave,
Your voice, a melody, gentle and brave,
"Hello," you greeted, a spark in the air,
"Ki re, ki khabor," words you dared to share.

Amidst the hustle of office's embrace,
We carved out time, a precious space,
Conversations flowed, a river of words,
Unveiling stories, like songs of birds.

Before our first meeting, in that exchange,
Love unfolded, free from constraint or gauge,
In the cadence of our voices, a promise found,
Echoes of our first call, in hearts tightly wound.

5. Autumn's Prelude

After our first call, a new chapter unfolded,
In the rhythm of our words, our story molded.
Daily, you sought my photos, my smiles to see,
A bridge of images, connecting you to me.

Our conversations flowed, a blend of joy and haste,
In the swirl of daily life, moments embraced.
Our chats, like streams, flowed steady and true,
Though sometimes brief, they bound me to you.

September sighed its last, October tiptoed near,
Durga Puja beckoned, bringing spirits close and dear.
From Kolkata you journeyed, to Balasore's awaiting shore,
To celebrate, to revel, to share traditions and more.

As the countdown shortened, our hearts beat in tune,
Anticipation crescendoed, under the autumnal moon.
In that interlude of whispers and digital light,
We awaited our first meeting, where souls took flight.

6. Anticipation in October's Dawn

The 15th October dawned with a bustling blur,
A date confirmed, a moment both tender and new.
Your family's visit, a sight to concur,
In this dance of fate, my heart's both anxious and true.

Nervousness brewed as I paced with doubt,
First time a boy for marriage would come to my home.
With each trip to the washroom, I pondered the route,
Wondering if our paths might connect or roam.

Your message arrived, a sign that you were near,
Baba revved his scooty, anticipation alive.
The home was adorned, with warmth and cheer,
And I, in Maa's saree, readied to strive.

As the minutes drew close, my heart beat in time,
Dressed in my finest, hopes gently entwined.
Ready to greet you, this future undefined,
For today's the beginning of what we might find.

7. Curtains of First Glance

As Baba's scooty drew near, a whisper of fate,
Maa's command led me to wait inside,
The tradition of old kept me hidden, sedate,
While my heart raced to catch a glimpse I couldn't find.

From my porch, the curtains became a veil of dreams,
Hoping for a glimpse of you, yet seeing none,
Sent to side room, my nerves came apart at the seams,
I paced restless, for this day had just begun.

A vague outline of you, in white and denim blend,
Seated serenely, fingers tapping a slow, rhythmic beat,
As I, with jangling bangles, in my own way, was glad,
To share a secret glance, though our eyes never did meet.

Summoned at last, I emerged from my hiding place,
With polite greetings, I took my seat by your side,
The curtain of separation fell, revealing your face,
In that first moment, our worlds were suddenly allied.

8. A Glimpse of Tomorrow

The question-answer round began with polite grace,
Your parents inquired, and mine set the pace.
We spoke of our lives, each question a thread,
While curiosity wove through the words we said.

I darted to Maa, seeking her calm,
While plates of cutlets and kalakand warmed the palm.
Hesitation lingered on your side of the room,
Mine's insistence cut through the tension and gloom.

I stood near the door, directly across your chair,
Trying to gauge the boy now sitting there.
Then came a gentle nudge, a proposal made clear,
To share a quiet moment, just us two, away from here.

Plans were set for a journey, a date to unfold,
To City Centre's Food Court, where stories were told.
In maroon kurti, from past birthday's bright scroll,
With blessings and hope, we'd explore heart and soul.

9. Sunset Journeys: The Auto Ride Chronicles

We stepped into the auto, bound for City Centre's grace,
Sat side by side with a hand gap, in formality's embrace.
Sunlight wrenched the air, crystal clear skies so wide,
Breezes danced around us as we ventured on this ride.

"Ar bal, ki khabor?" you asked with a familiar ease,
Our conversation picked up, carried on the breeze.
I showed you Sambalpur, its streets and simple charm,
The auto's hum a backdrop to our unfolding calm.

At the Food Court, you bought us Coke can to share,
With a spotlight on your face, you seemed almost rare.
In white shirt and denim jeans, with sneakers neat,
You faced me with a smile that made the day complete.

You joked of being a stud, with a twinkle in your eye,
Yet your smile and kindness spoke without disguise.
We skipped our lunch for laughter, mimics, and play,
Our similarities seemed to bridge gaps along the way.

Different traits, yet our thoughts seemed to align,
In conversation's dance, our worlds began to entwine.
I suggested a long auto ride to show the town's pride,
You agreed with a grin, and we set out side by side.

We took a Phuchka break, savoring the tangy blend,
Through fields and temples, the river's bend.
From Sambalpur to the metro, a journey in your gaze,
My small town's stories, in your city's ways.

Your roots in Bargarh made the distance feel so slight,
Connecting our worlds, in the shared delight.
The traffic jam seemed endless, yet our postures aligned,
Our legs inclined, a mirror to the day's gentle kind.

As sunset bathed us in its glow, a blessing from above,
Sunlight danced on our faces, a moment to love.
In that warm, divine light, our spirits seemed to blend,
In the quiet of the evening, our hearts found a friend.

In that final stretch of journey, as day turned to night,
We shared a quiet moment in the fading light.
A boy from Kolkata and a small-town guide so true,
Our auto ride became a cherished memory for two.

10. A Goodbye in Transit

As we rode through the city's dusky veil,
You insisted I first, then you'd prevail.
Though I begged to drop you where you'd stayed,
You held firm, our paths in compromise swayed.

My home was our first stop, where we did alight,
You offered to pay, but I claimed the right.
A gesture of care, a hand's gentle try,
Hesitated, held back, though it wished to comply.

"Let Baba drop you," I urged with concern,
To skip the traffic's snarl, the slow return.
After some persuasion, you finally agreed,
A small concession, a compromise freed.

My parents greeted with warmth and cheer,
Maa offered water, her gesture sincere.
But your phone's ring, a reminder so true,
Of home's waiting call and parents' due.

You bade farewell with a quick, soft goodbye,
A moment of parting beneath the sky.
You mounted the scooty, legs crossed with grace,
In that instant, our roles seemed to embrace.

I felt like you were me in that fleeting ride,
A reflection of self, with emotions allied.
You looked back with eyes both hopeful and veiled,
A goodbye that spoke of futures entailed.

The scooty's hum faded into the night,
Baba drove on, a quiet flight.
I watched you leave, hope mingled with doubt,
Wondering what future paths would sprout.

When asked of us, I said with a heart's plea,
That we could be more than friends, just wait and see.
The feelings were right, yet uncertainty's shade,
Left me questioning the path we had made.

The hardest goodbye was a moment so fine,
A mingling of hope and the passage of time.
With mixed feelings, I watched as you went away,
Hoping for more, come what may.

11. The Unspoken Verdict

In the shadow of uncertainty, a message appeared,
You'd reached the hotel, my thoughts all veered.
A day of result loomed, an interview's fate,
Balasore would reveal it, but still, I must wait.

The night was a spiral of questions and fears,
You headed to Balasore, through the restless gears.
Morning brought whispers, and noon dragged along,
The answer eluded me, as hours felt wrong.

Time stretched in slow motion, from dawn to the eve,
The answer a mystery, my mind did not cleave.
Evening gave way to night's gentle embrace,
Yet the answer I sought remained out of place.

Then, a message at 8:30, you'd arrived safe and sound,
Balasore was reached, but the answer wasn't found.
Your joke, "Ki re sunlam naki, tui biye pagla
hoyegechis?"
I replied "Tumi o toh," lost in confusion's abyss.

12. Echoes of Yes: February's Fate

It's Yes, a truth I missed amid the jest,
Baba's evening walk, a peaceful quest.
The message reached me late, his return the key,
The call from your side was lost in time's decree.

A call from yours, a message lost in flight,
For evening's veil obscured the moment's light.
An invite received, a chance to bridge the gap,
But tradition's grip held me in Sambalpur's lap.

Though eager was my heart to cross the miles,
Yet fate's design kept me from distant styles.
You asked me to join, but hope met with delay,
In vein, I wished to travel, but stayed where I lay.

On February's 10th, our path was gently set,
With horoscopes aligned, our fate was firmly met.
Ashirwad exchanged, our future now entwined,
In love's embrace, our hearts forever bind.

13. Kolkata Beckoned

Our marriage was set, a moment of cheer,
In Balasore's embrace, the venue was clear.
As days passed by, through messages we'd weave,
Plans for our wedding in WhatsApp's reprieve.

You chose your kurta and ordered a grand sherwani,
While I pondered my choices, both elegant and swanky.
Our outfits must match, in color and grace,
You suggested a journey, to find the perfect place.

In Kolkata, we'd shop, side by side in the fray,
Your mother spoke with mine, set our way.
The festive season beckoned, December's embrace,
I'd stay with my Mashi, as we prepared for this space.

With travel arranged, our excitement took flight,
To Kolkata we'd go, in the glow of December's light.
Our journey was booked, our hearts were aligned,
In this vibrant city, our dreams intertwined.

14. Reverie at Sunrise

Kolkata beckoned with its vibrant charm,
We spoke of shopping, roaming, and the grand plan,
To capture moments for our pre-wedding film,
Your family dinner invite, a gesture so warm.

With office closed for Christmas, you took a break,
As I and Maa packed, the journey we did undertake,
Through the train's rhythm, the landscape would reveal,
Your presence awaited, a welcome so real.

On Howrah's platform, amidst the rush and the steam,
You helped with our bags, like a guardian of dreams,
In the taxi, you guided, pointing out sights anew,
The Howrah Bridge, the morning market, the Ganga's serene view.

A flutter in my chest as we crossed the river's span,
A feeling so surreal, that I could barely understand,
You dropped us at my Mashi's with a friendly goodbye,
Leaving a trace of magic, as our hearts did sigh.

15. City of Joy: Magical Yuletide

On December's chill, after you left Mashi's grace,
I took a quick nap, in my quiet space.
You messaged your plans, office work to unwind,
By afternoon's grace, our meeting was aligned.

In the meantime, I ventured with Maa and Mashi dear,
To a jewelry shop where the day disappeared.
Payment delays kept me captive till dusk,
You called to check in, urging me to wrap up.

With the jewelry quest complete, I texted you then,
You waited outside Binayak Enclave, a patient friend.
I rushed past Mashi's teasing, eager to see,
You asked if I'd eaten, concern plain to see.

On a toto we traveled, to Monginis for a bite,
Your eyes showed worry, my hunger in sight.
Plans were postponed, you dropped me with care,
At Binayak again, asking me to message when there.

The next day's plan was lehenga shopping in cheer,
Your Parents, Maa, and I in a cab so near.
You took the metro after guiding your kin,
At the shop, your support was a comfort within.

In the lehenga trial, your care did shine,
"Are you comfortable?" you asked, so kind.
A maroon lehenga chosen, elegant and bright,
With another to match your sea-green light.

In trials of reception sarees, with joy we did partake,
You yearned to see me in yellow, a vision to awake,
Two sarees with stones, their shimmer soft and bright,
To complement your royal blue suit, a dazzling delight.

After the lehenga and saree hunt, we slipped away,
To Hoppipola for snacks and a future's sway.
We laughed and dreamed, in festive delight,
Then Westside for shopping, your gifts felt so right.

A black trouser, a pullover, and sneakers so white,
"Wear these tomorrow," you said with delight.
I was dropped back at Binayak, a heart so true,
The next day, in your gifts, I was ready for you.

You smiled at my new look, a joy so clear,
We roamed Kolkata, Trincas for lunch, my dear.
Pictures and laughter, a hairband you chose,
Our next day's outfit, a ritual that rose.

Toto rides and metro trips became our dance,
In Kolkata's Christmas cheer, we took every chance.
Through the city's lanes, our love danced free,
In December's embrace, just you and me.

On December 25th, beneath the winter's grace,
We met again, after a day apart's embrace.
I wore the sheath dress you gifted, soft and fine,
And wandered with you down Park Street's crowded line.

Christmas Eve, the city's pulse alive,
In chaos, we were swept, yet we would survive.
Amid the rush, your guard became my shield,
A tender grace where warmth and care revealed.

Your left hand on my shoulder, right hand too,
Protected me from every storm that blew.
In that embrace, my heart began to race,
Nervousness dissolved in your protective space.

The following day, a family meal to share,
Your kin awaited, and you showed such care.
In formal suit and green, you stood so grand,
Welcoming me with a touch of your hand.

I wore yellow and white, a chudidar's grace,
You said, "Bhalo lagchis," with a loving face.
You played hide and seek, capturing light's play,
As we posed for pictures in a joyful array.

Your relatives arrived, a gathering warm,
You hosted with poise, with gentle charm.
Conversations flowed like a family's tune,
In your care, I felt a sweet, safe cocoon.

Dinner concluded with smiles all around,
Your cousins snapped a photo, love profound.
You placed your hand on my shoulder so near,
In that snapshot, perfection was clear.

In every moment, in every touch you gave,
A tender gesture, a heart so brave.
Amongst the hustle, amidst the busy scene,
Your presence made every moment serene.

As we shared those festive hours, so dear,
Your care and warmth wiped away all fear.
In the chaos and the calm, in every frame,
Kolkata's courtship wrote a loving name.

December 27th dawned, our last day to roam,
In a rickshaw's gentle sway, the city felt like home.
You spoke of your Mashi's praise, how they were impressed,
I felt like a vision, in the city's embrace, blessed.

You took me outside your office, under the open sky,
Insisted I pose, while moments flitted by.
To the Mela in front, where colors danced and spun,
And a Rajasthani fair across the road had begun.

You warned of the time, urged we must be fast,
Yet fate had its own plan, a detour we amassed.
In the auto, you turned, a U-turn you chose,
To show me the other fair, where enchantment rose.

In the cab, your hand found mine, a touch so warm and kind,
My hand grew hot, yet your warmth I did find.
My phone slipped away, in the rush of our shared space,
An awkward moment, but your touch I still embrace.

You dropped me at Mashi's, where goodbyes started to loom,
Our last hours together, the air was tinged with gloom.
The next morning, you returned to help with my things,
A brief farewell, your presence a comforting ring.

At Mashi's, you met her family, formal yet sincere,
Your words were measured, with a gentle, caring cheer.
I escorted you out, our parting so near,
The last of our moments, tinged with a quiet tear.

At Howrah station, as evening did fall,
You guided us through, to the waiting room's hall.
You helped us find our seats, amidst the bustling crowd,
Our Kolkata courtship was ending, both tender and proud.

The train's siren echoed, marking our final scene,
You waved until we left, your farewell bittersweet and keen.
As the train departed, my heart ached with strain,
The absence of you left a lingering pain.

In the stillness of my berth, the train's gentle sway,
Tears traced my cheeks, for the end of our day.
I laid there sobbing, feeling a loss so profound,
Already missing you, as the wheels spun round.

16. Beneath the Wedding Veil

In Sambalpur, where the town whispered cheer,
Wedding bells began their chime, so vivid, so clear.
Our journey back was more than a mere return,
It marked the start of plans, each corner a new turn.

Cards were printed, each design a loving detail,
Blouses were measured, tales of fabric would unveil.
Invitations fluttered with hopes and dreams entwined,
As parents orchestrated plans, two families aligned.

Through chats and video calls, our hearts grew near,
You wished me New Year's cheer as midnight drew near.
Fireworks danced on your terrace, a shimmering light,
In those moments, our bond grew ever so tight.

A message flashed, "Toke anek miss korchi," it said,
Left me breathless, thoughts of you swirling in my head.
"Ar kichudin, tarpor tomari kache," I sent back in kind,
Time seemed to stretch, yet you remained in my mind.

Days trickled by, with anticipation building high,
You and your family went to Balasore, as time flew by.
In Sambalpur's warmth, my Aiburobhat did gleam,
In a blue saree with maroon border, I was a dream.

Maa's feast was a marvel, with dishes so fine—
Rice, pulao, dal, bhaja, and fish in a line.
Chicken curry and mutton, with sweets galore,
Payesh, misti doi, sandesh, kalakand to adore.

Yet the jest of the feast, though tempting and grand,
I'd savor it slowly, each bite planned.
I shared the photos as you wished, so fine—
Your "Sundor lagchis" made the moment truly mine.

A celebration in every way, so bright and true,
With love and laughter, I cherished it with you.
We prepared to follow, our hearts set on the venue,
Travera packed with our hopes, our arrival would be
true.

On February 3rd, we reached, with dreams in our sight,
You sent the location, guiding us through the night.
Your parents welcomed us, their smiles warm and bright,
But you were absent, caught in your office's plight.

I waited with eager eyes, scanning through the crowd,
Hoping for a glimpse, my heart both soft and proud.
In the busy blur of life, I yearned for you to appear,
But in the rush of your world, I held our moments dear.

My parents journeyed to your ancestral home so true,
To extend the invitation, with hearts warm and new.
On February 8th, from the break of dawn till late,
The mehendi ceremony began, with designs ornate.

Adorned in a green lehenga with a red dupatta's flare,
I had the first letter of your name traced with care.
Yet when I asked the mehendi didi about your own,
I learned you were not keen, felt a sadness shown.

Despite the disappointment that lingered in my heart,
I kept my feelings to myself, not wanting to impart.
As evening fell, you asked for photos, so I sent,
You video called, and we spoke, our bond was spent.

We shared our smiles and words before the call was cut,
Your cousins arrived, and we ended our virtual rapport.
As the days of festivity unfolded, our hearts intertwined,
In the ebb and flow of wedding prep's, love defined.

17. A Symphony of 'I Do'

On the morning of February's 9th day,
We moved to a nearby haven where our kin would stay.
Relatives arrived in their vibrant array,
The prelude to our grand engagement's ballet.

In the parlour across from the venue's grace,
I donned a sea-green lehenga, a smile on my face.
With a messy bun and hopes like the sky's hue,
I waited in the venue's hall, where moments would ensue.

Your arrival was heralded by my cousin's cheer,
First came your two Pishi, their warmth so clear.
Then a fleeting moment when you appeared,
Our eyes met briefly, a memory endeared.

Elders bestowed blessings with Arati and Tika bright,
Gifts in hand, their warmth filled the night.
Rings exchanged and cake cut in the soft light,
Photos and laughter under stars' gentle sight.

Though my three-inch heels made dancing a feat,
Your heart swayed freely, making the evening complete.
You danced with a fervor, a rhythm so sweet,
In that joyful moment, our spirits did meet.

The grand day dawned on the 10th of February,
A golden mark on life's radiant tapestry.
From early morn, the 'Dodhi Mangal' rites began,
Adorned in Sankha Pola, as my journey ran.

Maa's eyes glistened with a quiet sorrow,
As cousins teased and jests began to flow.
I hurried to the parlour, amid laughter and cheer,
To ready myself for the Gaye Holud's sincere.

Women of my kin, with conch shells' sweet sound,
Went to the pond, where traditions abound.
With a Diya aglow and water pure in brass,
They brought the essence of the past to the present's
clasp.

In a yellow saree with a red border fine,
I joined the Vriddhi Puja, where spirits align.
Baba, with reverence, sought ancestral grace,
For a life filled with love, in our sacred space.

Turmeric's embrace from your side did come,
A paste and a saree, with gifts for what's to come.
Bathed in pond water, in a cascade of gold,
Moments captured in chaos, a story unfolding bold.

After the turmeric bath, with golden light I gleam,
Rushing to the parlour, like a bride in a dream,
In maroon lehenga, woven dreams in crimson hue,
With maroonish pink dupatta flowing like morning dew.

A white topor graced, a crown of pure delight,
Wooden sindur daani cradled, a symbol of sacred rite,
Dupatta tucked with grace, a dance of tradition's call,
Kalka on my forehead, where ancient blessings fell.

Amid the hustle and bustle, the excitement was rife,
Photographers clicked away, capturing moments of life,
One dear friend arrived with gifts to share,
As the barati came, filling the air with their flair.

Mashi, Mama, Mami, cousins tried to keep me confined,
Before Subho Drishti, I mustn't see you, they reminded,
Rituals commenced and you were welcomed with cheer,
Joyous sounds of ululation and conch shells drew near.

Maa came with Baran dala and sweets so sweet,
Performing an Arati, making the moment complete.
The atmosphere sparkled with festive delight,
As I stepped outside, fluttering with a mischievous plight.

There you were, a glimpse of joy through the crowd,
Before a cousin's jest pulled me back to the shroud,
In this vivid tapestry of love and lore entwined,
You, my beloved, in beauty so refined.

In stages of light, solo pictures were taken,
Moments of grace, each frame finely shaken,
While rituals called under Chadnatolla's shade,
Potto Bostro came, and memories were made.

The mandap stood ready, its elegance pure,
For Subho Drishti, the moment we'd endure,
With 'Din Shagna Da' playing softly in the air,
I began my walk, a sight beyond compare.

Carried by cousins beneath a floral arch,
Betel leaves shielded, a sacred and bright march,
Mashi and Mami teased, "Don't peek through the side!"
Yet I caught glimpses of you, with joy amplified.

Your broad smile was evident, a beacon of light,
As I circled you seven times, in pure delight,
You watched with care, ensuring my path was clear,
In my heavy lehenga, your love drew near.

As the rounds completed, I unveiled my face,
Our eyes met, and smiles lit up the sacred space,
With happiness shared, laughter in the air,
We exchanged garlands, our hearts laid bare.

Rajnigandha and roses, symbols of our vow,
In front of all present, we made our promise now,
The first step as partners, a journey we'd start,
In the mandap, our lives intertwined, heart to heart.

After Mala Badal, our path led to Bedi's domain,
Where emotions ran deep, like a tender, gentle rain.
Baba placed my hand in yours, a heartfelt embrace,
The 'Sampradaan' complete, our new journey in place.

In that sacred moment, numb yet full of grace,
Our hands tied with thread, hearts quickened their pace.
The priest chanted mantras, the fire's glow was bright,
We took Saat Paak around the flames, a timeless rite.

Seven betel leaves beneath, our journey now begun,
In the holy fire, our vows sealed, spirits fused as one.
Puffed rice from my cousin, a gesture rich and true,
Together, we cast it in flames, our hopes and dreams anew.

You held my hand with care, guiding it with grace,
In the Yagna's blaze, our love found its place.
Sindoor Daan marked our fate, red sindoor so bright,
A new saree veiled my face, our hearts' pure delight.

You adorned me with bangles, a bond's vibrant hue,
I became 'Mrs.,' as our love grew.
In this dance of life, our journey started anew,
As Mr. and Mrs., with love ever true.

From this day forth, our paths were one,
In every glance and touch, joy had begun.
A union forged in fire and thread, in love's eternal grace,
We walked as one, forevermore, in life's embrace.

After completing rituals, we posed with pride,
Newlyweds with parents, joy as our guide.
Your parents now mine, mine now yours too,
As husband and wife, a life to pursue.

We dined with delight, sweets and dishes we shared,
Fed each other lovingly, moments declared.
Then to cousins we went, their laughter so bright,
Basor Raat's warmth, a festive night.

Games with the young ones, songs that were sung,
Antakshari played with hearts ever young.
Together as a team, in merriment we soared,
No rivalry here, just joy we explored.

As dawn approached, the farewell was near,
With heavy hearts and a tearful veneer.
Leaving 'Mayer Bari', my past left behind,
Journey to a new home, a future defined.

Two cousin brothers joined us, gifts in their hands,
In a flower-decked car, with heartfelt plans.
Through tear-filled eyes, you tried to bring cheer,
With clumsy words to make my sadness disappear.

Arriving at your home, puja and prayers we gave,
At your ancestral temple, traditions to save.
Changed from wedding attire, took a brief nap apart,
In separate rooms, a moment to restart.

Daylight brought 'Mukh Dekha', gifts from your kin,
In their loving presence, new beginnings did begin.
Lunch on the terrace, cousins all near,
Maa, Mashi, and cousin came, their warmth sincere.

Rushed to the parlour, with your Pishi in tow,
In a stoned yellow saree, I glowed in the show.
You in a blue suit, amidst gifts and cheer,
Photographs captured, moments so dear.

We celebrated until dawn, in joy we basked,
The terrace alive with laughter unmasked.
'Kaal Ratri', a night for rest and retreat,
In separate rooms, our tradition complete.

The whirlwind of functions, so hectic and bright,
Wove our bond strong in the midst of the night.
Through rituals and laughter, our life did commence,
Creating a lifetime of love and immense.

In the quiet dawn, our hearts beat in sync,
The first day as one, where dreams did start to link.
With laughter and light, we explored gifts and trinkets,
In a room that was ours, where love found its pickets.

You, on leave from the world, beside me, so near,
We shared whispered moments, with joy crystal clear.
I draped myself in the red dhakai's embrace,
Sankha and Sindoor marking the sacred space.

Our First Night, soft and sweet, a tender embrace,
In a pink saree and flowers, I felt our hearts' grace.
You, in white kurta, beneath a bloom-filled space,
Gifted the Mangalsutra, gold's gleam brightening our
place.

I offered my poem, in tender tones and heartfelt rhymes,
A gift of words shared in the quiet night's chimes.
The evening held a secret, in a wistful glow,
A quiet wish for a hug during our Sambalpur auto's flow.

In that quiet, heartfelt moment, with the city's gentle
hum,
I felt your deep affection, how our hearts had truly come.
Your affection spoke softly, clear and true,
In that simple instant, our bond shone through.

In marriage's fresh embrace, all was new and unknown,
New faces and customs, a world I had to own.
As I navigated this change with uncertain air,
You stood close, my friend, with unwavering care.

18. The Dawn of Us

In a new home where love's seed had been sown,
I stepped softly, my heart now their own.
Maa and Bapi, I cherished the role,
Striving to nurture, embracing each soul.

Through laughter and care, our bonds gently grew,
In the warmth of their presence, I found something true.
With each day's effort, my heart did align,
As a daughter to cherish, in love we did bind.

In the quiet dawn of our new life, I found you near,
A husband so caring from the very first day here.
You learned what I loved to eat and what I wore,
With tenderness, you'd never let a single mosquito soar.

You couldn't bear to see my tears or my pain,
In every moment, you stood by me through sunshine
and rain.
We shared meals, laughter, and life's little scenes,
Our days passed by like cherished dreams.

'Ashtamangala' came, the eighth day after our vows,
My parents were at your Balasore flat; a special house.
We visited, stayed just a day, then returned with a smile,
For Shivratri brought puja at your ancestral shrine.

That brief stay was filled with newness and grace,
You made an effort to warm up, to find your place.
You began to break the ice, like a son in their eyes,
A bond was forming, and it felt like a prize.

After they left for Sambalpur, we lingered a while,
Working from home, we explored with style.
Chandipur's beach and Radhakrishn temple were our first outing as one,
Walking hand in hand, feeling the warmth of the sun.

On Chandipur's sands, you kissed my head so light,
A flutter of butterflies took flight.
You spoke softly, lying beside me in bed,
"Today I felt like I too have a family," you said.

In Balasore's kitchen, my first payesh was a start,
Then chowmin, crafted with heart, served as a snack.
Though you ate slowly, you savored each bite,
Like flavors anew, each bite made the effort bright.

To Digha Beach, we journeyed with a cab so bright,
For two days of seaside joy, and ocean's light.
Though you hesitated, fearing the waves' playful spree,
I walked away in frustration, but you soothed me
tenderly.

Soon we laughed in the surf, side by side in delight,
Capturing moments of joy, our hearts took flight.
With every splash and embrace, our worries did cease,
In the rhythm of the waves, we found our shared peace.

Life was steady, and our bond was true,
But love was a realm I longed to pursue.
We were friends and partners, a husband and wife,
Yet love's confession was still out of sight.

One day, in a casual chat, you made a surprising claim,
"I don't believe in love," you said, causing me some pain.
I valued love deeply, wanted it to stay,
So I paused and countered, "But pure love is my way."

Our first Holi came, colors danced in the air,
Amid your jokes and laughter, love was everywhere.
Even when unintentional hurt came my way,
You wiped my tears and made me feel okay.

Then came the time to visit Sambalpur's crowd,
A reception party with photos and blessings allowed.
We sought divine grace at Huma Leaning Temple,
A pleasant stay, where joy was ample.

Maa and Baba welcomed you with warm embrace,
They saw you as their own, your place in their space.
You grew comfortable with them, as they did with you,
Our family bond strengthened, in ways we never knew.

Returning from Sambalpur, we faced a new phase,
Kolkata awaited us with its bustling ways.
A car journey with parents, from Balasore we drove,
Hybrid work culture began, as our new chapter roved.

To Kolkata we journeyed, hearts full of dreams,
Where joy and the Ganges wove endless streams.
In bustling streets and whispers of old,
A new chapter of life together did unfold.

19. Bonded by the Ganges

Kolkata, the City of Joy on the Ganges so vast,
With Maa and Bapi, we stepped through the past.
At the door, Maa brought a kalash so bright,
Arati essentials in a ceremonial light.

She applied a tilak, so gently to us both,
With blessings from Maa and Bapi, we took an oath.
I tilted the kalash with rice, full of grace,
A coconut cracked, marking our new place.

You held my hand, excitement in your eyes,
Showing me the rooms, where our new life did rise.
The balcony and terrace, our space to explore,
A shelter for joy, as we settled in more.

I sorted your things, from mess to serene,
Turning cluttered chaos into a tranquil scene.
In each tidy space, our lives found their beat,
Creating a haven where harmony and order did meet.

Days turned to weeks, our life began to blend,
From 'The Boys' era to 'The Husband' trend.
Your gym machine stood firm in our tiny space,
Your passion intact, no need to replace.

I knew you were doubtful, a hint of dismay,
But I said, "Leave it, it's here to stay."
Your smile grew wide, reflecting your cheer,
A loving exchange, so sincere and clear.

In weekends, we roamed through Kolkata's charm,
Trincas was our haunt, where we found calm.
You held my hand, guiding through the street,
Protecting me always, your care was sweet.

In Sundarban's embrace with Maa and Bapi dear,
We savored a staycation, drifting without fear.
A ferry ride through tranquil waters so wide,
Nature's splendor unfolded as we sailed side by side.

In Sundarban's mangroves and wildlife's domain,
I faced my period's discomfort amid nature's reign.
Among the tangled roots and the forest's deep call,
Your gentle care supported me through it all.

Through my period's ache, you stayed through the night,
Dozing beside me, a comforting sight.
Your presence a balm for my pain's deep refrain,
Offering solace through each throbbing strain.

Returning, I looked pale, burdened by the ache,
Yet you found solace in a gesture so great.
At a bus halt, you sought out a nearby grove,
Plucking raw mangos, a loving act to prove.

Despite the gardener's slangs and his dismay,
Your thoughtful act brightened my weary day.
With each mango you gathered, a smile you'd restore,
A tender reminder of love at its core.

Whenever I was out, your worry would rise,
A veil of tension veiling your eyes.
You'd watch and wonder with anxious dismay,
Your care and concern never straying away.

One day, with Maa and Bapi, I went to visit,
Your Mashi in the hospital, amid your work blitz.
Before I left, a small argument made us part,
Your calls and texts revealed your anxious heart.

You rang twenty times, messages tenfold,
In panic and anger, your worry took hold.
Silent phone beneath the bag, I couldn't reply,
Returning home, I calmed you, love in our eyes.

Life moved on, with its sweet and crunchy finesse,
Balancing joy and challenge in its tender caress.
May arrived, with your birthday in sight,
We planned a journey, to Balasore's delight.

A relative's wedding, a celebration in tow,
Our journey was more than just a show.
Through ups and downs, our bond remained tight,
In Kolkata, our love continued to ignite.

Your smile and care, in every little act,
Filled our days with joy, never lacked.
From the kalash to the mangoes, and beyond,
Our life in Kolkata, a cherished bond.

In Balasore's embrace with Maa and Bapi near,
We came to celebrate your birthday and wedding cheer.
For the first time, I'd orchestrate a day so bright,
A heartfelt tribute to you, my beacon light.

20. Those Three Words

In the rush of 2nd May's dawn, with rituals in play,
Maa and I were swept in the ceremonial ballet,
You, encased in meetings, bound by your chair,
While I prepped surprises with a devoted flair.

Gifts of joy stacked for days, a birthday parade,
T-shirts and toy guns, in loving charades displayed,
Two cakes were ordered, a red velvet delight,
And chocolate to follow, a double treat in sight.

Yet chaos arrived as Maa and I were entwined,
The delivery called, a sweet moment misaligned,
You bound to your desk, unable to assist,
I raced through the sunlight, a hurried twist.

The cakes received, chilled in the fridge with care,
I returned to the venue, a worn-out affair,
With time slipping fast, and functions to attend,
Decorating our room became the task to transcend.

Balloons to inflate, confetti to scatter wide,
A 'Happy Birthday' banner for which I had pried,
The foil curtain to hang, lights to aglow,
A birthday surprise, where love was to show.

Amid the whirlwind, you noticed my strain,
My weary face, the exhaustion, and pain,
You urged me to rest, in your concerned embrace,
But duty and love drove me to complete the space.

Dinner and events, a quick return to our nest,
An hour left to perfect, to give you my best,
Blue and silver adorned, a spectacle to see,
With every detail placed with a loving decree.

You were sent away, while I worked through the night,
Transforming our room into a birthday delight,
Midnight struck, and with it, the heartfelt cheer,
A celebration for you on 3rd, and a love sincere.

The cakes were cut, and we fed each other sweet,
In the glow of the room, our hearts did meet,
Parents' blessings and laughter filled the air,
With selfies and smiles, we cherished the affair.

Lying close as the day began to unfold,
In the quiet of the night, as stories were told,
You whispered softly, your love to confess,
Three words in the dark, in a heartfelt address.

"Shon na," you began, with a voice full of grace,
"Ekta Katha Bolbo – I LOVE YOU" embraced,
In that sudden whisper, my heart took flight,
Love affirmed in the silence of the night.

The weight of your words, in the quiet of dreams,
A confession of love, more precious than it seems,
My hard work and struggle, now softened with grace,
As we laid side by side, love etched on my face.

In a moment so sudden, I hugged you tight,
With mixed feelings swirling, my heart took flight.
Your words, unexpected, pierced through my guard,
Confessing love when my emotions were marred.

I couldn't return those words with a clear voice,
Though my heart felt a tumultuous choice.
I asked you repeatedly, "Say it once more,"
Seeking reassurance, a truth I did implore.

In the morning's chaos, the wedding's grand spree,
You wore the T-shirt and jeans gifted by me.
Amidst the celebration, you chose to remain
In that simple attire, avoiding the plain.

While I dressed in a saree for the evening's delight,
You stayed in your same T-shirt and jeans, a stubborn sight.
Obsessed with the outfit, you chose to defy,
The planned attire, as moments slipped by.

Returning to Kolkata, things felt redefined,
Your love had been confessed, yet I lagged behind.
Days turned to weeks, and my heart felt unsure,
With my response to your love still obscure.

When others would jest, with laughter and chatter,
Jealousy surged, and I'd bother and smother.
My heart was unsettled, a storm of dismay,
As I struggled with love, day after day.

Possessiveness grew as each day slipped by,
As I struggled with feelings I couldn't deny.
It wasn't a single instance but a recurring phase,
Of wanting you solely, through love's complex maze.

Though you confessed your love in a moment so pure,
I wrestled with feelings, unsure and unsure.
Yet my own tangled emotions clouded my view,
As I grappled with feelings both old and new.

In time, I hoped to express what I'd yet to reveal,
To mirror your love with a truth that was real.
For now, the memories of those days held sway,
A testament to the love that guided my way.

Amidst the dawn of summer's gentle grace,
We set our sights on Darjeeling's high embrace.
A honeymoon in those mist-clad peaks we planned,
With the allure of mountains, soft and grand.

In late May's warmth, we flew the azure skies,
My first flight was a thrill, with excitement in my eyes.
I gripped your hand tight as we soared above the sea,
A world of clouds beneath, with you beside me.

Upon Bagdogra's ground, our journey began,
A cab ride through the hills, as nature ran.
With Google's guidance, we sought out our stay,
A cozy retreat where we'd rest and sway.

For two days we booked, with hearts light and true,
A trial of comfort in a place new.
And as days unfolded, our contentment grew,
We chose to extend our stay, and asked if we could too.

But fate, with its whimsy, had its own plan,
A call from the hotel stirred a dilemma span.
Our room was pre-booked on a date unforeseen,
We'd need to find a new place, it seemed.

In the dark of night, with rain's quiet song,
We ventured out, where shadows did belong.
Our umbrella faltered, its frame awry,
Yet you held me close beneath the stormy sky.

With trembling hands and rain's chilly breath,
We walked Mall Road, through damp and depth.
Your warmth shielded me from the night's embrace,
As we searched for solace in that wet, misty space.

Yet in the morning light, our stay was renewed,
The hotel's kindness in our hearts imbued.
We rode the toy train to Ghum's quaint scene,
And strolled to the zoo, where wonders convene.

In traditional garb, we posed and we played,
Captured moments in love's tender cascade.
On our final eve, under Darjeeling's twilight,
You whispered "I LOVE YOU" with a heart's pure light.

As we packed our bags for the homeward flight,
Darjeeling's charm lingered in our sight.
A journey of romance with its trials and cheer,
A memory cherished, forever held dear.

As days passed, your yearn grew strong,
A desire to hear "I love you" all along,
Whenever we ventured into the world outside,
Evil eyes stirred arguments, emotions did collide.

Tiny quarrels sparked by shadows unseen,
You longed for those words, pure and serene,
One day, amidst our heated strife,
You spoke of the wish that danced through your life.

Calmness embraced me as your words took flight,
I'd planned a surprise, on my birthday's night,
Just waiting for the perfect time, so grand,
Your smile brightened, softening the land.

Laughter bubbled, a secret I had let slip,
Yet our hearts' desire was an unbroken grip,
June arrived, and with it, the day to honor,
Maa's birthday, a celebration to ponder.

We adorned the room with joy and cheer,
Balloons and banners, our love sincere,
The cake was cut, family photos captured,
In that moment, a heartfelt bond was enraptured.

As we laid side by side in gentle repose,
I whispered close, where tender love did flow,
"Shon na, Bolte bhari ichhe hocche," I confessed,
Your response was gentle, leaving me impressed.

"Bole de, don't wait for moments grand,"
You urged, "Let the moment be as it stands,"
Your words broke the silence, opened the gate,
For my heart's true message, no longer late.

"I LOVE YOU," I said, with earnest glow,
"I LOVE YOU MORE," our emotions did show,
The sky above and our hearts intertwined,
In Kolkata's hues, our love so defined.

21. Beyond the Last Page

Today is a weekend, a gentle pause in time,
Memories and musings intertwine and climb,
I sit on the balcony with a cup of black brew,
As I pen the final lines of our poem, just for you.

You lounge in the armchair, persistently asking,
But I tease you with a smile, gently masking,
"Suchi, what are you doing? Show me, please!"
"It's a surprise," I say, hoping to appease.

We've journeyed some kilometers from where we began,
With endless miles ahead, life's uncertain plan,
Each step a new chapter in this unpredictable tale,
Where paths twist and turn, and dreams set sail.

A small-town Bengali girl with a Master's degree,
In Sambalpur, self-reliance was my creed, wild and free,
Now married to a CS boy in Kolkata with Balasore's ties,
Our love's serendipity, where my heart truly lies.

We linked through Bargarh, a shared past,
In this small world where our lives were cast,
Your school there, my B. Tech close by,
A connection forged under Odisha's sky.

Just 65 kilometers, yet worlds apart before,
Now joined by love, destiny's encore,
You from one town, me from another, entwined,
Our hearts linked so swiftly, a bond that's defined.

In the tapestry of time, our journey's spun,
One and a half years, where love's colors run,
It's not just smiles but tears that have found,
A blend of sweet and bitter, both profound.

The lavender whispers of romance's grace,
Mix with the fire of jealousy's embrace,
Yet through every flavor, every hue and scent,
Our hearts find a rhythm, together content.

In moments of sorrow, and days of delight,
You are the chapter that makes my life bright,
The sweetness of love and the depth of our plight,
All weave into a story that feels just right.

God wrote our love in the stars above,
A script of passion, of trials, and of love,
You are the most beautiful verse in my fate,
A masterpiece crafted, both tender and great.

I adore how you love—life, family, and me,
Your boundless affection, a treasure to see,
I love you deeply, with mind, body, and soul,
Your love makes me whole, more than I could have told.

You loved first, but my heart fell harder still,
Even on days I struggle, your love fulfill,
Daily, I find new ways to love you and thrill,
With each sunrise, our bond grows stronger, we instill.

You are my anchor when my strength is thin,
I love you more than anything, through thick and thin,
We lift each other's dreams, both in work and in heart,
Nurturing growth together, never drifting apart.

Proud to be your wife, in all that we've become,
In this shared journey, our love's the outcome,
Daily, I fall for you in new and profound ways,
It's been one and a half years of shared, cherished days.

As only child, we once lived with choices all our own,
In solitude, our desires and paths were fully known,
Yet now the irony in our love gently unfolds,
I give up my lower berth while you trade your window's hold.

In our shared moments, these gestures softly speak,
Of how love transforms our lives, making us complete,
From solo decisions to our tender swaps in kind,
Our gestures weave a bond that's heartfully entwined.

Through every shift and change, we've blended well,
A puzzle complete, our love's tale to tell,
Beyond the final page, where forever dwells,
Our love's infinity, in each other, we excel.

As I sip my coffee, and you wait with bated breath,
I reflect on our journey, love's depth,
In every chapter, every twist and heft,
Our love's the constant, the gift that's left.